Breakfast in Memphis

Vol. 1
Universe Favors the Hero

Mark Randall Mueller

Cover Art by Analy Nakat

ISBN: 979-8-9885322-3-1
EBOOK ISBN: 979-8-9885322-0-0
Library of Congress: 9798988532231
Cover Art by Analy Nakat
Instagram: @analynakat
www.analynakat.com

Breakfast in Memphis: Universe Favors the Hero

Dedicated to my sons, Max and Andy, and the empowerment of a new generation of heroes fueled by love and seeking truth and justice for the benefit of all.

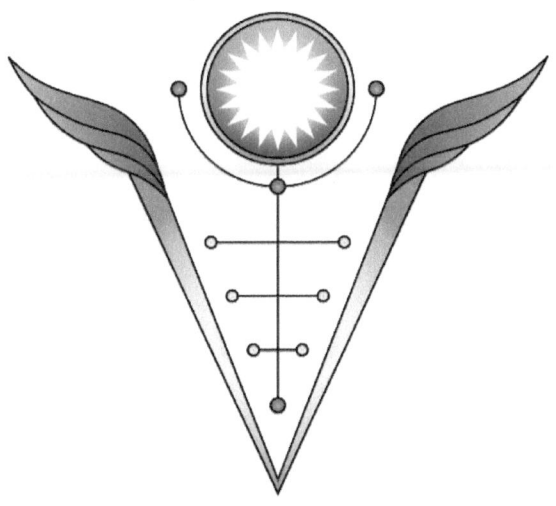

Truth and Justice League was founded from the realization that we live in an unjust and badly contaminated world and that without a positive vision for the future and the participation of ordinary people, destruction of the human species is inevitable. In the summer of 2019 we hosted a special event called the What if? Party to connect with and inspire a community of scientists, doctors, lawyers, journalists, filmmakers, environmental and social justice activists, churches, regenerative agriculturalists, artists, musicians, educators, healers, and many others to combine in their own unique ways to create a more sustainable, equitable and peaceful world.

Cont'd...

Do well by doing good. It is important to remember we are here to live free, pursue happiness and avoid hurting others through violence, carelessness, greed, toxic exposure, fraudulent business practices, discrimination, prejudice or hate.

Truth and Justice League's mission is to assist in the creative evolution of the legal system to improve the balance of fairness and justice in the lives of all people. Join us in becoming part of the solution. Let's build a better future, together we rise!

FOREWORD

The title poem for this first volume of the <u>Breakfast in Memphis</u> poetry series, <u>Universe Favors the Hero</u>, was written for and inspired by my twin sons, Andy Hays Mueller and Max St. John Mueller. Remarkable musicians and even better human beings, they have taught me so much about the power of love and resilience.

Like many families, our lives have been tumultuous, challenging, and on more than one occasion, terrifying. We have shared several near-death experiences, hospitalizations, arrests, accidents and injuries. Together, we've gone through harsh, prolonged, expensive divorce and custody battles, deep and years-long separations and many levels of loss, pain, chaos, and confusion.

Our survival code became the phrase, "in the blood." Against all odds, in the darkest of times, we told ourselves we would somehow manage to survive and find a way to achieve our dreams.

I was blessed with amazing parents, Doc and Pat Mueller (ages 95 and 94 as of 4/17/23). They are loving, saintly, and supportive. They provided me a safe, stable home to grow up in, and for that I am grateful. My own wounds were self-inflicted. My path to self-awareness is ongoing and I am grateful that my sons and I have survived our own family journey and are now able to share music, poetry and messages of lessons learned with audiences in need of hope, inspiration, love and spiritual connection.

The title poem is an acknowledgment of the ever-increasing challenges my sons' generation is facing due to the

Cont'd…

warring, toxin polluting, greed worshipping, unhealthy, and unbalanced world we have left them. They are now being called upon by spirit to perform at the very highest levels, under the most adverse and damaging physical and mental environment of my lifetime, and perhaps, of known history. If they, and others, are able to summon the inner hero then maybe, just maybe, they will find the key to unlock a better future for at least one more day.

What if?
We bypassed the fear
And ignored the confusion
And do what we can do now
Without worrying about
The rest of it
Or what others have done
Or will do
And without giving any power at
All to those known or unknown
Who seek to block us, diffuse us
Defeat us or mislead us,
What if?
We started this today?
No ego, no shame, no regrets
No winners or losers
Or too small or too old
This is a co-ed team
Whatever that means in
This day and age

Gender, race, politics, religion
Educational degrees, resumes and achievements, past trauma
Past lives, personal history
Family problems, bank accounts,
Debts and credits
Leave them in the locker room
They just weigh us down
And divide us
If you need a uniform one will be provided
You pick your own number, symbol or name

Who wants to play?

Cont'd...

Breakfast in Memphis: Universe Favors the Hero

The field is open
I've got a ball
Keep it simple
Have fun
Like when we were kids
Imaginary is real
We have energy
And health
We are young and strong
There are no limits
Who wants in?
Say when

Aho

Wizard Bear Speaks
Breakfast in Memphis

Warning 18+

This collection of poems contains adult topics, explicit language, raw emotional content, imaginary worlds, and harsh examination of self and others including many political/religious/corporate and government agencies.

Universe Favors the Hero

Universe
Favors the hero
No time for regrets
Fuck all excuses
One chance is all you get
One is all you need
No doubts
Be brave
Stand up
Shoot straight
Yes you
You know
It's in the blood
It's in the mirror
I'm looking at you
You're looking at me
I'm looking at me
You're looking at you
When the end is midnight
Heroes know
To die not trying
Is not living anyway
Take the chance
Find the key
Unlock tomorrow
And the world goes on
Another day
Universe favors the hero

Breakfast in Memphis: Universe Favors the Hero

Constant Conflict

Is it the road to understanding
Or some kind of peace
The apparent insolvability
Of things

Which can't be mentioned
Aren't seen, yet seem real
Partial puzzles, great unknowns

Fill in the riddle
The mind fills in blanks
Guesses turn to believing
Small pieces still missing
Sometimes lost
Forever
What were they
What could they possibly mean
Confirm or conceal

How lucky we are

Forever changing
From one cage to another
Our personal zoo

Natural landscapes
Depend on the weather
Internal designs
Yet no written label
Misleading meanings
Is a human design
Increasingly lost?
Or right on time?

Nice summer stories
Of green leaved
Beliefs
Turning brittle and brown
Dying in paradise
Creating the next round

Holy Ghost

Holy Ghost walked right into my sleep
Said sometimes My son
You got to roll the bones
But don't you worry baby
It don't help anyway
The Holy Ghost voice
Was deep and black
And from somewhere in north Mississippi
I guess this was a religious experience
Or maybe I just went bat shit crazy
I think that Atlanta trial just
Got a little biblical
Kaleb for the win

Uneven Steps

Uneven steps
In the house of the Lord
Winding down stairways
To places unknown
Feeling the way
When the light wasn't there
Perils in alleys
Basements that stare
The ceiling is lower
And cracked with decay
What musty old tombs
Of my past lives
Were abandoned
Here
Buried in dust
Often unshared
Better sometimes
To leave them this way
The light is much better
Upstairs with more space
To make even better mistakes

Solstice Sacrifice

In the crosshairs
Of my life
I took aim
A quarter past midnight
Living on borrowed time
Pulled it back
Held it steady
A single string
One flaming arrow
Sliced the night
Down went the
Target right
On the mark

My Morning Coffee

Black, strong, hot courage
Sounds like a girlfriend's dream
I fill my Merit metal cup
Do my two minute Toltec practice
Facing east,
Two hands above the chin Bringing in future feeling
Of when this current challenge is resolved
For better than imagined
I must be crazy
Charlie? Am I crazy
Uni, Babycakes and Corky?
Am I crazy
A council of friendly, exotic creatures woven of cloth and string
Wearing tiaras, diamonds, and rubys,
Jester hats and New Orleans earrings,
French scarves
African ties
And a medicine bag from Chuck in Tyler
How many lifetimes
Have I done a similar dance
Or is that all make believe
And bullshit from well meaning
Healers who speak
A different language
One that I do not understand
The construction noise of the
City goes on every day
Building higher and higher
With scores of brown workers
From who knows where
This is the daily struggle
To find the path and see the meaning and purpose of
What to do today
And how to
Create the future
That lies beyond
This day and time
Ya mon … Aho

Breakfast in Memphis: Universe Favors the Hero

(Tic Toc Toltec Rolling Back the Clock)

Passing through
Midnight from the other side
Of time
Unwinding the trauma
Back before pain
Before the betrayals
Broken relationships
Loss, disease
...So much guilt
And shame
Winter to fall
Summer to spring
Wash away time
Being I am
Without the bullshit
Lies and blame
"Ya mon"

Code Black

Forget what you know
Drop what you can
Get ready to move
Quickly without wasted
Motion
And no mistakes
The surf is rising
Sharks in the water
Sun is going down
New moon rising
Midnight surfing
Might as well be
Blind…death is waiting
All around…
This where…
The treasure may
Be found…
Odds are long
So what
Time is short
Good
Then why
Waste time
We walk the edge…
It's what we do
Midnight surfing
Enemy territory
Can't see you
Anyway

Come back with the missing key
Unlock the door for
One more day

Viking Dreams

Cold rain
Wakes me early
Today will be
The day
Land of many rivers
Codes and marks
On faded maps
Tales from drunken sailors
Illuminate the way
Stacks of gold...
Long lost treasure
Hidden not far
From sight
Finder keeps the gold
Brave and lucky
Sailors
Paying
Attention
To dreams
Of a young man captain
Secret sea to shore
Passage
A land beyond the water
Reward for risk of life
The gold pays

For the journey
And public failure
Redemption was worth far more
Viking gods are calling
Find the unknown land
You dreamed about
Since maybe three or four
It's true,
You somehow know
What you seek
But cannot see
Is what you're fighting for
Lightning strikes,
Clear dreams calling
Dark seas uneasy...
Danger all around
There's no cute little mermaids
Swimming round below
No one here to save you
But all you need is you
Viking gods speak truth
This you can believe
If only you can hear it
You were born for this
I know

Antidote

*Medicine chest
*Breath of hope
*Conquering fear

The paralysis of fear
Is immediate, vicious, crippling,
And just fucking annoying
Kneecapping dreams
Intent on destroying
The remedy you hold
Is in your own medicine chest
The one that holds your heart
And breath
The one located about 18 inches
Below your fear jacked head
Parachute, stumble or elevate down
Take back your breath
And get out of the crown

Ya mon

Burial of a Friend

Do I have
To hate you
When it's me
That forgot to notice
I was standing on
A make-believe corner
Of an intersection
That didn't exist
That traffic light
Changed years go
Before I knew
Your name
Nothing that came
Before or since
Changed the nature
Of that game

Follow the Moon

Walking the night
Through my stolen city
Dancing around misery
Government ink
And fear
Rivers of darkness
The smell of piss
Death Valley shadows
Brick and glass canyons
Tall buildings
Block out
The sun
Leonard Cohen's
Dead voice
Now reminding me
"Without light
There are no shadows"
Carry on

Munchausen by Proxy

The game you invented is no fun to play….
Trauma to trauma
Always a crisis
Usually more than one
Escalating emergencies
Headlong into chaos
Coming undone
Victim or martyr
Same deadly disease
Calls for attention
Emotional 911
Then just at the last moment
You become a hero
As if by design
And once again all is not
Lost
Till the next time
And the next time
Exhausting your friends
And yourself even more
The gravestone says
Munchausen by proxy
If that's what you want

Jane Henry

Get off the bus
Close the chapter
Shake off the dust
Reweave that old
Coat
Of damaged
Wool
That kept you alive
When you wanted
To give up
Take all you've learned
Expand your heart
Grow new wings
Blossom can fly
So can you

Damaged Wool

The value of
Sacrificial lambs
Is woven
In our fabric
Are you
One of god's
Chosen ones?
Inserted into
Epic Tragedy
To react and spin

Damaged wool
Recording it all
In great detail
The real history
Branded
Damaged
Resilient
Allowing others to see

Occult Moon

Clouds in the midnight sky
New Orleans
Moon over Masons
32nd degrees
Fuck you

Papa Legba calling
Griffins, Crows,
And ravens
Jester king daddy got
More work to do

1000 Crows

Were calling
From atop
A federal building
Downtown New Orleans
May 29 twenty twenty-two
What were they
Trying to tell me?
Voices beyond the grave
Hale Boggs name was
On that building
Warren commission
Wrong side of Hoover
Was the beginning of the
End
Skydiving without a parachute
Alaska wilderness
Ya mon
A message from the other side

Virgins or Cuckholds

Man of God
Trapped in a prison
Of our own beliefs
Banging on the doors for the keeper of keys
Guard will you rescue a victim
From self-inflicted disease
Lord help me Jesus
Get up from the floor
One day soon Mother Mary
Gotta open that door

Government Ink

A harsh tattoo
Branded like cattle
Stained much deeper
Skin to bone
Labeled
And shunned

Ridiculed and
Avoided

Scarlet and black
Flashing neon

What they say
You become

Hard choices
Roads not traveled

Broken hearts and
A fallen soldier
Two young daughters
A wife
And a lover
All
Tattooed
In government ink
False history
A convenient
And unbelievable
Story

Of lone nut
Commie ex-soldiers
In all our schoolbooks
Life Magazine

Cont'd...

Breakfast in Memphis: Universe Favors the Hero

And TV
News reporters

Yes you too
Dan Rather
Speaking lies
For CIA bosses
The company line
Was make-believe

You reassured a
Nation of willing fools

That 6th floor corner
Window
The gun
The shells
The lone assassin
None of it was true

From a graveyard
Near Dallas
Lee is the
Whisper of wind

Semper fi
Semper fi
A good marine
Till the end
But who and why
And what does it matter?

The credits and characters
Scroll down like a movie

Producers
Writers
Directors

Cont'd…

Editors
Executive/co-producers
Actors
Cameos
Soundtrack
Crew
Grips
Makeup
Disguises
Bullets
Weapons
Security
Marketing
Funding
Accounting
Distribution
Commissions
Blue ribbon panels
Congressional blessings

Blame it on the devil
So many faces
And too many names
Johnson, Nixon, Bush, Tolson
Dulles, lawyers and cops, secret service real and imposters,
Mafia/CIA/military gunmen and leaders, Bay of Pigs survivors,
Hit men, soldiers of fortune, Cubans, Watergate burglars, Hoover, McCloy,

And so many others...who made the profits
Who gained the power
Who sealed the documents
Kept killing for silence
Buried for decades
Redacted or just gone

A nations betrayal
We pretend we can't

Cont'd...

See

Neutered and
Pickled
Kept in a jar
A nation without
Balls...heart...brains
Or even a mirror
Here we are now
America the great
Broken by lies
Branded by treason
I'm out of the game

Dedicated to Judyth Baker and Lee Harvey Oswald

Social Media/Modern Marketing

Fear based
Click bait
Cancer, vax
Covid, mandates
The war machine
Needs more
Money… honey
Hear those bitches
Roar
Basket full
Of titties
Dick pics…
Or rolling dice
You too can be
A millionaire
Just click here twice

Requiem for a Virus/End of the Pandemic

Then one day it happened
People forgot
To be afraid
They said fuck you
To fear and doubt
Remembering to be alive
Is more important
Than worrying about
Your death
Ya mon
Remember to be alive
Death comes soon enough

Commander in Dreamland

Mr. Tyrant sir, fake leader, orange liar,
President/commander, whatever
Who exactly are you
And who are you working for
If you knew anything about me
Or the world itself
You wouldn't be such a waste of
Oxygen
And now it's just too late
Is the mirror in your house broken?
Did bad mommy spank you too?
Was it all those private schools?
Learning the rule of gold
And not the golden rule
Is that why you're
So greedy
And untrue
Sshhhh it's ok now baby
It will be alright
Just come this way
We can help you
You're so misunderstood
Poor little orange one
Its not your fault
The game is not the same
As you imagined
When daddy made the rules
You're tired now...so tired...
...Shhh...you...need...
To…go…to…sleep
Bye bye little baby
No more command for you

McRaven

Mr. McRaven,
Mr. MD…
GOT A BLACK HAT, mask and glasses so
No one can see
Protected from virus and killing disease
Life and death borders just lines on a map to me
The direction you go
Is all up to you
Don't think too long about death
Or delight though
The intersection you stopped in
Is the truck lane
You know

Increasingly Obvious

Wherever you look
Distractions
Clickbait
Nip pics

Fox News
CNN
Yahoo
Facebook
You name it
Nukes
Vaxx
TikTok
China
AI
UFO's
Trump trials
Biden wars and scandals
Censorship, controls
Misdirection,
Rich man's tricks
Masks and games
Trans shooters attack with guns
Bud light/crack pipe
Fentanyl/Narcan
Send your damaged ones to
The left run cities
Mix in street drugs
Guns, free tents
And some Nazi's
Let the games begin

Cont'd...

Breakfast in Memphis: Universe Favors the Hero

Now the Dalai Lama
Shilling for booster shots
And suck my tongue
In the heart of madness
The patterns are revealed
LoveTruthJustice
Magnify and shine the light
People get ready
Universe favors the hero

Gratitude

For being here
And a chance
To feel
See
And learn
A chance
To love
A chance
To sing and dance
A chance to live
In paradise
And a chance
To walk in grace
May we each
See truly
What ONLY WE
Can do
To save
This magic
Kingdom
From toxic
Overdose,
Mind control,
Greed,
Rape
And murder
That tarnish
And destroy
The golden
Glow of
Paradise
Implanted in our
Souls

Now

Look back
Slowly
Only
To see
How far
You've come
Return to
The present
Moment
Now
Get on
With living
The best
Has just
Begun

Aho

Someone May Be Watching You...

But do they know your name...
In the world of constant observation…
The details get to be confusing...
And all roads look the same...
When you say hello to your government...
Make sure to tell 'em fuck you...
And where to spend their time...
Make sure they write down your name...
And identity...
So they can keep better track next time
Fuck you Facebook, Google, app tracking corporate
Government
You couldn't survive a week
Where most people come from
What makes you think you know better
How to live their lives,
If you had wanted to be helpful
You had plenty of time
Better spend your money on the way down
Or you'll share the same charcoal grave

Forgotten Sundays

Your mother failed you badly
She shoulda kept you locked inside
The basement playing those video games
Your bank account is hemorrhaging ego
But who taught you how to dress,
Was daddy a Brooks Brother's
Vampire who fucked a camping world
Clown
On forgotten Sunday's only
Your bookie knows whether you're in town
Your megachurch preacher from Dallas
Is pleading with his Christian god
Please help those Dallas Cowboys
Be again America's team
Dear God, I pray just one more coach a
Good one please
Philadelphia is Lucifer's special team,
Devil Eagles beating God's own Cowboys
At a football game
Must be the Antichrist
Praise the Lord
This second coming better include
A first-round pick

God of War (and Football)

Praying to win
God's team?
By law we are all equal...
By nature we are part of the same...
What God created now he wants to be killed in his name?
Against all enemies foreign and DOMESTIC...
In God we trust...
Cause we can't trust us...
That's why Jesus moved to Vegas...
Takes cash...pays credit, sells timeshares
In Heaven...
Vatican Bank
Commodity broker
Forgiving sins
Laundering money,
Ashes to ashes
Dust to dust

Now Mother Mary listen up...

Brown Waters

Another rising tide
In our sea of bullshit
Where volume passes for
Meaning
Talk talk talk
And never listen
Smart or dumb just
Shut the fuck up
Your Phi Beta Kappa
Alibis and reasons
Destroyed your own
Defense
Four taps of a
Velvet Vanderbilt
Hammer
Silver nails
To a wooden cross
Phi Beta fuck
You
Next time
Use the solid gold
Ones melted
Inside your head.

Mormon in Houston

Meet you in the temple
Of secrets and lies
Unsaid... Unforgiven
Controlling the show
Darkness and light
Sworn to believe
The church is true
Devil's got the 5 o'clock
Shadow
Mother Mary does too

Little Tin Soldiers

Bankers and lawyers
Your time has come
Lies, guns, and money
All coming undone
Get out of the shadows
Stand in the light
Truth to power
Wake up everybody
Choose wisely
This is permanent ink
Final exit coming
Only one way out

Behind the Mirror

Behind the mirror
Is a box
Of treats
Sugar, cigarettes
And beer
A shivering chihuahua
Crawled out of bed
Sweet dreams baby
Turned into nighttime dread
Rottweilers, dog pounds
Unhappy masters
Locked up
Abandoned
Needing to pee
And shit
Tired of running
Don't wanna play fetch
Collared, neutered
Constant distress
Feed me a biscuit
I'll do any trick

Transition

Chihuahua was tired of
Shivering and dreamt now
Of a better life...
He was tired of feeling small
And afraid...
And wondered if a better life was even possible...
And if so how to find it...
He has always admired the
Larger, more powerful dogs
Pit bulls, German shepherds,
Great Danes, mastiffs
Shit even the bassets, wieners and beagles outranked his little
Mexican ass
He began to wonder what it would
FEEL like to actually BE
A larger more powerful and confident breed...
He decided to skip the wieners, bassets, and beagles
And go for a nice mid-range
Breed like a boxer or bull terrier
He closed his eyes and imagined he now was a handsome brindle
Boxer
Distinctive, muscled, and sleek
As the warm sun of his imagination soaked in
He sure felt good...
Walking around town
Tall and strong was
Amazing
Everyone looked at him
Differently now
No more people making fun
Of his yappy bark
And insecure bravado
Now it was what a handsome boy you are
And wow, isn't that a cool looking dog, is that a boxer?
This was better than a warm
Meal on a cold day

Cont'd...

Breakfast in Memphis: Universe Favors the Hero

That felt so good why stop
In the middle?
In quick succession he shapeshifted in his mind to
Great Danes, rottweilers and
Mastiffs
Damn this was good shit
Clear a path, get out the way
Does he bite? Oh he's friendly
Wow, what a gorgeous dog
This was really good shit indeed
So why stop at the big breeds
Why be a dog at all…
Why not a big cat…a leopard or tiger or even the king
A golden maned lion
Once again the warm sun
Of his imagination
Followed his intent
A magnificent king lion
With five queen lionesses
In a fabulous pride
This imagination is real
Shit sure is good stuff
Better get a kilo
So I never run out
He wondered
What if a lion could have wings?
To fly to the mountains
And even the beach
And so it was, little shivering
Chihuahuas became the legendary griffin king…
Now human
It's your turn to
Imagine
A better dream
Let's see what you can do
Aho

Wake Up Little Chihuahua

It's no time for fear
Today you're a griffin
With silver wings
A lion's mane
And a mission
You've done it before
You can do it again
No barking excuses
No trembling in vain
You got shit to do
Shake off that madness
And fly off into the rain
Head for the sunshine
The view is much better
Those wings have a purpose
You'll know what to do

Masters of Profit

Can you hear IT
The hungry rumble
War machine needs
MORE
Something on the horizon
Maybe you can't see it yet
But soon it will be at the border
And next year living next door
Invisible enemy
Media? You keeping score?
Wake up the stories
To be retold again
Got to be patriotic
Defend our way of life
Our right to be spied on
Our right to be deceived
Got to defend the homeland
Democracy stands for freedom
The American dream baby
Washington's elected generals
And the lucky one of us
That gets to be the president
When the war machine needs money
You know
It's a priority
The war machine needs
Money
I said
Money
More
More money

Congressional Report

Hold on to your shorts
Don't spill your drinks
You won't believe this
But it's true
I swear
Congress finally did something right
And it's important…
Someday and Funday
Are now official days of the week
It is being debated whether the 7-day week will be extended to
9 days
Which would complicate the calendar and zodiac signs
But slow down aging...
Or whether
The two new days will replace the currently existing
But less popular days
Such as Monday and Thursday
Additional changes are possible
And being proposed
As competing bills
Make their way through the outdated
Corrupt and suffocating halls of
Congress
One radical caucus
Is moving to do away with the concepts of
Time and
Calendars all together
Citing accumulating new scientific evidence that
Time is not linear and perhaps not real at all
Moneyday and Sinday are two of the more popular
Alternative or additional names and/or days of the week
Being considered

Breakfast in Memphis: Universe Favors the Hero

Tyler Tea

Ambassador's Kool-Aid
Is tasty
I know
Believe me
I drank some
Before
You
Were born
Each sip
Gets you high
On vanity and pride
Good luck
Young rangers
The enemy
Wasn't me
It's Carrier, Trane,
PPG
And all of the
Industrial polluters
Trying to get off
That hook
And escape scot-free
Tumbling dice
Not pretty
Not nice
The cost of
Tuition
Play to win

I'm your Huckleberry
Say when

Silver Dollars

Silver dollars fell from heaven...
The tax man saw it rain...
The churches got their deductions...
For praying in Jesus' name...
The military got funds for weapons...
But God was on our side...
The Church of Politics decided who would gain...
Halliburton and Lockheed made profits...
Patriotic mothers cried tears...
For real soldiers...
Who lost their lives in vain...
A suicidal mission...
In the master profit game...

Breakfast in Memphis: Universe Favors the Hero

National Security

Leave our people alone...
We don't need you anyway...
And we never have...
You always waste our time...
Go protect a Walmart...
Or guard a cash machine...
At least we wouldn't have to pay you...
To waste our fucking time

Breakfast in Memphis: Universe Favors the Hero

Heavenly Dice

God and Satan
Shooting craps
In the alley
Folks were gathered
Round
Christians praying
For deliverance
Bookies making odds
Mobsters and churches
Taking skim
The game went on
And on
Money kept changing
Hands
The odds were in
Our favor
But then the devil won

QAnon Commands

Yoga sisters
Breathe and Listen
Woken and rising
Dice with Roger Stone?
Words of cryptic code,
Evil masters
Pedo zoos

Cruz control
Numbers and colors
Orange Julius
Hang tight with
Drag queen Rudy

Oh Giuliani please...

Keyboard warriors
Holy shit, motions, and briefs

Sounds like war
Call the court
Praise the lord
Help me Jesus

Dominos fall like summer rain

Vanderbilt J.C.
Trump U MBA

Liberty Law JD

COVID preemptions
Fake elections
Hanging chads

Banging heads

Cont'd...

Polling stations

Constitution
Guarantees
The right to be

Mind-fucked

Meme-sucked

And padlocked
Libtards, Trumpets
Ghostbusters, Klan
Stand and
Pledge allegiance to

To God's chosen one

The Giant Staypuff Man

One day is all it takes
Credit for time served
Come and get your law degrees

Printed fresh daily
Fed Ex/Kinkos store
Right between Gap and Apple
Make a left at the food court
Near the escalator
On the second floor

Supreme Court lessons
Clothes and gadgets

Fake degrees, guns, and badges
All right here and waiting
Down at old Highline mall

Sonic Medicine

Sonic alchemy
Musical blueprints
For a new existence
Gifts of unknown gods
Far away worlds,
And ancient places
Passed through time
Sent by the future
Audio calibrate
Soul adjustments
Musical theory
Mathematical
Forms

Genetically coded
And passed on to
You
By countless generations
And centuries of time

Sonic messages
Couldn't be any clearer
Best team required
No time to explain
All of them know
Follow the sounds
Listen for more
Messages for heroes
Mission is calling
Your journey is here
And only beginning
Others will find you
Familiar feelings
Wearing different faces
The road you seek
Leads you now to unseen places
Good luck
Fellow heroes

El Dorado

Golden hair, silver tongues and witches
This must be El Dorado
Black robes, altars, thrones
And Bibles
Holy shit it's Sunday
Time to go to church
Guess again it's Monday
This is trial court
Hand on the Bible
With the other one raised
When sworn
Means the lying is just about to
Begin.
Veritas verdictis
Truth gets fucked

Puppets and Lies

The price of life
Despite the discount
Is high
Where do you
Go
When the cost is
Your pride

Golden Line

Golden line baby
Dominos falling
Like summer rain
The path clears itself
Sunshine guides
The way
Ya mon

In the Dawn of the Long
Dark Day(dream)

Where fools are kings...
And slaves are leaders...
The awake ones by silent agreement...
Formed a secret nation...
Conceived in liberty...
And born from injustice...
I see the fools and slaves...
I prefer the lucid dreamers...the artists...dancers...workers...
Magicians and those that care and sing...
To a secret nation...it's been here all along...
People get ready...

Show Me the Way

Daylight is coming
Bring me my life
Show me the way
To become who I
Am
I'm tired of confusion,
Fear
And avoidance
Pretending, guessing
Lies, ego
And so much wasted time
May it be so for me
And also for you
Aho

Plastic Jesus

Plastic Jesus
Mother Mary
For God's sake
And man's

Get out of the doorway
You're blocking the sun

Eternal Rangers

Keeping watch
Will they
Turn
In your direction
Ask and you
Shall receive
As above so below
Ask for help
In your direction
Ya mon

(Don't Give Up)

Living on sunshine
And borrowed air
Then one day
You look up
And see the
Treasure
Just lying
There

Apollo 13/Update

Houston...are you there?
You, on Earth, have a problem
It's a big one
Humanity is on the brink
The planet and its inhabitants
Have been poisoned
Lied to
And controlled
For a very long time
The deceptions and methods
Are ongoing, expanding
And accelerating
This is an existential/spiritual/scientific crisis
Humans are being required to perform
At their highest levels under the most adverse
Physical and psychological health conditions
Everyday heroes are essential
And we must trust
That universe does favor the hero
Aho
Prayers for us all

Empty Pocket

No telling what you might find
In an empty pocket sometimes

Inside every hero
Is a child who
Wasn't good enough
In their own eyes

No one ever
Knows
What another has
Been through
Or what lies
They told themselves
To survive

No telling what you can find
In an empty pocket sometimes

Another Day in Paradise

Another day in paradise
Is about to unwind
What kind of magic
Can we build in
By design
Our shivering chihuahua
Becomes a griffin in disguise
Flying with the dragons
High above us
In the skies

ABOUT THE AUTHOR

Breakfast in Memphis Vol. 1: The Universe Favors the Hero is the first in a series of poetry by Austin, Texas and Atlanta, Georgia trial lawyer, Mark Mueller. "Several years ago, these words just came into my head, unpredictably, late at night, early in the morning, while walking in downtown cities, in times of isolation, pain, loss, disappointment, crisis, love, regret, awe and joy. They often seemed to almost type themselves onto my cell phone or iPad, usually perfectly formed and complete, sometimes in pairs or bunches, and slowly they accumulated into Breakfast in Memphis."

Mark Mueller is recognized for his work in birth injury litigation and product liability cases involving damages from unsafe medical devices, chemicals and pharmaceuticals. His work has twice led to FDA safety advisories for both vacuum extractors and vaginal mesh, and then eventual removal of many dangerous transvaginal mesh devices from the market.

He successfully represented the Brave Dog Society of the Blackfoot tribe in preventing oil and gas development in a pristine national wilderness area of Montana. Mark is also counsel for the Lakota

Cont'd...

Sioux Sundance Chiefs regarding ownership rights to sacred ceremonial objects.

A number of his precedent setting, high profile cases have been featured in the national media including, most notably, Oprah, Good Morning America, Special Insider Edition, The New York Times, Texas Lawyer and National Law Journal.

Mark's production company, Voodoo Cowboy Entertainment, hosted annual musical and art performance parties for many years. Through his production company, he also served as associate/executive producer for independent films including *Downloading Nancy* (Sundance Festival), *Winter in the Blood*, *Slam Planet*, *The Two Bob's*, and Ed Brown's environmental documentary, *A New Resistance*. He was a featured speaker and panelist for Conscious Media Festival programs on topics of sustainability and creating positive culture change.

Mark is currently developing a comprehensive and innovative legal strategy and support network called the Truth and Justice League. The goal of the Truth and Justice League is to address the nation's disastrous environmentally toxic legacy in ways that will hold wrongdoers accountable and lay the foundation for a more sustainable future. The hope is to restore personal freedom and democracy through active citizen involvement, jury trials, and a more informed and participatory voting public.

Mark is also the author of Unicorn Park, a children's poetry book, Breakfast in Memphis Vol. 2: Midnight in the Desert and Breakfast in Memphis Vol.3: Colors of Love.

ABOUT THE ARTIST

Cover Art by Analy Nakat
Instagram: @analynakat
www.analynakat.com

Analy Nakat is a full-time artist living in Los Angeles, CA working in various mediums including painting, drawing, collaborative projects, tattoos, and music. A native of Lebanon, her family fled war and relocated to the state of Texas when she was 13, where she struggled to assimilate into American culture. At the age of 18, Analy left Texas and moved to the San Francisco Bay Area, where she studied illustration at the California College of the Arts

Her haunting, often surreal work is revealed through a magical world that incorporates images of women, animals, plants and the patterns of nature, all of it suffused with a fascination with anthropology.

"Seeing how diverse people can live, and how people can adapt, I try to create magical places where people live in harmony with nature on canvas."

Find other volumes in the Breakfast in Memphis series here:

https://www.truthandjusticeleague.com/books

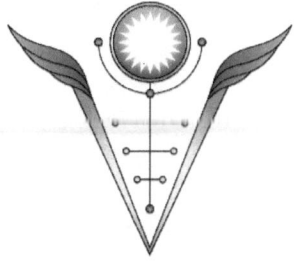